Math Tables You Need

Go-To Solutions

By William J. Saunders

Table of Contents

About This Book

Here's a Go-To book containing those hard-to-find conversion and help tables when they're needed. Whether it's for cooking, gardening, shopping, or a household project, this is a source you can use.

But remember, the information is general and may not apply exactly for a given situation. Consider that and consider safety. Always consult with professionals when in doubt, and / or when safety is involved.

1   Decimal Equivalents

8ths	Dec	16ths	Dec	32nds	Dec	64ths	Dec	64ths	Dec
1/8	0.125	1/16	0.062	1/32	0.031	1/64	0.015	33/64	0.515
1/4	0.250	3/16	0.187	3/32	0.093	3/64	0.046	35/64	0.546
3/8	0.375	5/16	0.312	5/32	0.156	5/64	0.078	37/64	0.578
1/2	0.500	7/16	0.437	7/32	0.218	7/64	0.109	39/64	0.609
5/8	0.625	9/16	0.562	9/32	0.281	9/64	0.140	41/64	0.640
3/4	0.750	11/16	0.687	11/32	0.343	11/64	0.171	43/64	0.671
7/8	0.875	13/16	0.812	13/32	0.406	13/64	0.203	45/64	0.703
		15/16	0.937	15/32	0.468	15/64	0.234	47/64	0.734
				17/32	0.531	17/64	0.265	49/64	0.765
				19/32	0.593	19/64	0.296	51/64	0.796
				21/32	0.656	21/64	0.328	53/64	0.828
				23/32	0.718	23/64	0.359	55/64	0.859
				25/32	0.781	25/64	0.390	57/64	0.890
				27/32	0.843	27/64	0.421	59/64	0.921
				29/32	0.906	29/64	0.453	61/64	0.953
				31/32	0.968	31/64	0.484	63/64	0.984

Numerator / Denominator

Examples:

1/8 = 0.125

1/4 = 0.25

1/2 = 0.5

2   Extension Cords

Length	to 10 Amps	to 15 Amps
to 25 Feet	16 Gauge	14 Gauge
to 50 Feet	16 Gauge	14 Gauge
to 75 Feet	14 Gauge	12 Gauge
to 100 Feet	14 Gauge	12 Gauge

Wire Gauge required for sufficient Amperes of Current from Power Source to the Unit requiring Power

For example:

If the unit to be Powered requires 10 Watts, the Extension Cord must be able to deliver 11.5 Amperes of Current.

Why?

Current = Voltage / Power
115 Volts / 10 Watts = 11.5 Amperes needs to be delivered through the Extension Cord.

3 Fractions

8ths	Dec	16ths	Dec	32nds	Dec	64ths	Dec	64ths	Dec
1/8	0.125	1/16	0.062	1/32	0.031	1/64	0.015	33/64	0.515
1/4	0.250	3/16	0.187	3/32	0.093	3/64	0.046	35/64	0.546
3/8	0.375	5/16	0.312	5/32	0.156	5/64	0.078	37/64	0.578
1/2	0.500	7/16	0.437	7/32	0.218	7/64	0.109	39/64	0.609
5/8	0.625	9/16	0.562	9/32	0.281	9/64	0.140	41/64	0.640
3/4	0.750	11/16	0.687	11/32	0.343	11/64	0.171	43/64	0.671
7/8	0.875	13/16	0.812	13/32	0.406	13/64	0.203	45/64	0.703
		15/16	0.937	15/32	0.468	15/64	0.234	47/64	0.734
				17/32	0.531	17/64	0.265	49/64	0.765
				19/32	0.593	19/64	0.296	51/64	0.796
				21/32	0.656	21/64	0.328	53/64	0.828
				23/32	0.718	23/64	0.359	55/64	0.859
				25/32	0.781	25/64	0.390	57/64	0.890
				27/32	0.843	27/64	0.421	59/64	0.921
				29/32	0.906	29/64	0.453	61/64	0.953
				31/32	0.968	31/64	0.484	63/64	0.984

Numerator / Denominator

Examples:

1/8 = 0.125

1/4 = 0.25

1/2 = 0.5

4 Insulation

Attic Insulation Recommendations

Zone	Region	Total on Floor
1	So FL	R25 - R30
2	Deep South	R25 -R38
3	South	R25-R38
4	Mid	R38
5	Mid North	R38-R49
6	North	R49
7	High North	R49

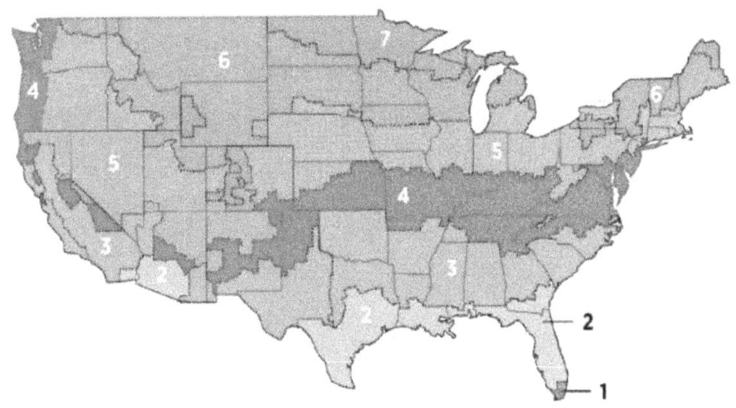

5   Lighting

Output	Bulbs Energy Usage in Watts		
Lumens	Incandescent	LED	CFL
200	25	3	
450	40	8	13
800	60	13	15
1100	75	15	25
1600	100	20	30
2600	150	28	35

Actual values vary among products

LED = Light Emitting Diode

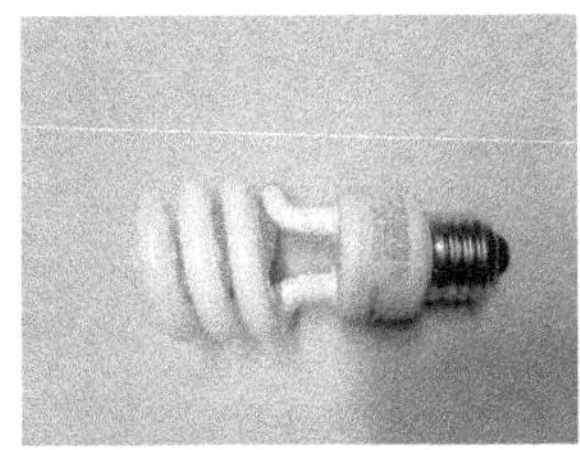

CFL = Compact Fluorescent Light

6 Linear Measure

US Standard	
12 Inches	1 Foot
3 Feet	1 Yard
5280 Feet	1 Mile
1760 Yards	1 Mile

Metric	
10 Millimeters	1 Centimeter
10 Centimeters	1 Decimeter
10 Decimeters	1 Meter
10 Meters	1 Decometer
100 Meters	1 Hectometer
1000 Meters	1 Kilometer

7 **Liquid Measure**

<u>Liquid Measure Conversion Chart</u>

Dash =	< 1/4 Tsp		
1 Tbsp =	3 Tsp =	1/2 Fl Oz	
1/8 Cup =	1 Fl Oz =	1 Tbsp =	6 Tsp
1/4 Cup =	2 Fl Oz =	4 Tbsp =	12 Tsp
1/2 Cup =	4 Fl Oz =	8 Tbsp =	24 Tsp
1 Cup =	8 Fl Oz =	1/2 Pint =	237 Ml
2 Cups =	16 Fl Oz =	1 Pint =	474 Ml
4 Cups =	32 Fl Oz =	1 Quart =	946 Ml
2 Pints =	32 Fl Oz =	1 Quart =	0.964 L
1/4 Quart =	1/2 Pint =	1 Cup =	8 Fl Oz
1/2 Quart =	1 Pint =	2 Cups =	16 Fl Oz
4 Quarts =	128 Fl Oz =	1 Gallon =	3.78 L

8 Metric Conversion

Inches	Centimeters		Centimeters	Inches
1	2.54		1	0.39
2	5.08		2	0.79
3	7.62		3	1.18
4	10.16		4	1.57
5	12.70		5	1.97
6	15.24		6	2.36
7	17.78		7	2.76
8	20.32		8	3.15
9	22.86		9	3.54
Feet	Meters		Meters	Feet
1	0.30		1	3.28
2	0.61		2	6.56
3	0.91		3	9.84
4	1.22		4	13.12
5	1.52		5	16.40
6	1.83		6	19.69
7	2.13		7	22.97
8	2.44		8	26.25
9	2.74		9	29.53
Yards	Meters		Meters	Yards
1	0.91		1	1.09
2	1.83		2	2.19
3	2.74		3	3.28
4	3.66		4	4.37
5	4.57		5	5.47
6	5.49		6	6.56
7	6.40		7	7.66
8	7.32		8	8.75
9	8.23		9	9.84

9   Nails by Gauge

Gauge	12 1/2	12 1/2	11 1/2	11 1/2	10 1/4	10 1/4	9	9	8	6	5	4	3	2
Inches														
1														
1 1/4														
1 1/2	4d													
1 3/4		5d												
2			6d											
2 1/4				7d										
2 1/2					8d									
2 3/4						9d								
3							10d							
3 1/4								12d						
3 1/2									16d					
3 3/4														
4										20d				
4 1/4														
4 1/2											30d			
4 3/4														
5												40d		
5 1/4														
5 1/2													50d	
5 3/4														
6														60d

10   Nails - Penny

Penny Nails	
<u>d</u>	Inches
2	1
3	1 1/4
4	1 1/2
5	1 3/4
6	2
7	2 1/4
8	2 1/2
9	2 3/4
10	3
12	3 1/4
16	3 1/2
20	4
30	4 1/2
40	5
50	5 1/2
60	6
70	7
80	8

In the U.S. Nails are usually sized in Pennies, or d (for denarius, a penny-like Roman coin) (for example, 4d, 5d, 6d, etc. are different lengths).

11 Roof Pitch Multiplier

Roof Pitch	Multiplier
2/12	1.01
3/12	1.03
4/12	1.05
5/12	1.08
6/12	1.12
7/12	1.16
8/12	1.20
9/12	1.25
10/12	1.30
11/12	1.35
12/12	1.41
14/12	1.54
16/12	1.67
18/12	1.80
20/12	1.94
22/12	2.09
24/12	2.24

Roof Pitch is the vertical rise in Inches for a 12 Inch horizontal distance.

For example, a 6/12 roof = a 6 Inch vertical rise for a 12 Inch horizontal distance.

12   Running, Swimming, Racing

Running

Event	Miles	Meters	Yards
Sprints	.06, .12, .25	100, 200, 400	109, 219, 437
Middle	.5, .93	800, 1500	875, 1640
Long	1.86	3000	3281
5K	3.1	5000	5456
10K	6.2	10000	10912
1/2 Marathon	13.1	21082	182
1 Marathon	26.2	42164	365

Swimming

Event	Miles	Meters	Yards
50	0.03	50	55
100	0.06	100	109
200	0.12	200	219
400	0.25	400	417

Horse Racing

Event	Miles	Meters	Yards
Sprint	Under 8 Furlongs		
8 Furlongs	1	1609	1760
9 Furlongs	1/8	1811	1980
10 Furlongs	1 1/4	2012	2200
11 Furlongs	1 1/38	2213	2420
12 Furlongs	1 1/2	2414	2640

13 Screws

Number	Diameter	Fraction	UNC	UNF
0	0.06	1/16		80
1	0.07	5/64	64	72
2	0.08	3/32	58	64
3	0.09	7/64	48	56
4	0.11	7/64	40	48
5	0.12	1/8	40	44
6	0.13	9/64	32	40
8	0.16	5/32	32	36
10	0.19	3/16	24	32
12	0.21	7/32	24	28
14	0.24	1/4	20	28
5/16	0.31	5/16	18	24
3/8	0.37	3/8	16	24

Machine Screws

UNC = Coarse Threads per Inch

UNF = Fine Threads per Inch

#	Diameter
0	1/16
1	5/64
2	3/32
3	7/64
4	7/64
5	1/8
6	9/64
7	5/32
8	5/32
9	11/64
10	3/16
11	13/64
12	7/32
14	1/4
16	17/64
18	19/64
20	5/16

Wood Screws

14 Sound and Decibels

Sound Measurements	
What	Decibels
Jet Engine	140 +
Pain	125
Chain Saw	120
Lawn Mower	110
Train	95
City Traffic	85
Vacuum Cleaner	75
Refrigerator	55
Whisper	25

Decibel Level Examples

Power (Watts)	Volume (Decibels)
1	87
2	90
4	93
10	97
20	100
40	103
100	107
200	110

**Power Driving an 87 Decibel Speaker
As Power doubles, Volume increases
by only 3 Decibels**

15   Temperature Conversion

Temperature Conversion	
Fahrenheit	Celsius
Degrees	Degrees
32	0
50	10
68	20
86	30
104	40
122	50
140	60
158	70
176	80
194	90
212	100
225	110
250	130
275	140
300	150
325	165
350	177
375	190
400	200
425	220
450	230
475	245
500	260

16 Volume Measure

US Standard	
1728 Cubic Inches	1 Cubic Foot
27 Cubic Feet	1 Cubic Yard
Metric	
1000 Cubic Millimeters	1 Cubic Centimeter
1000 Cubic Centimeters	1 Cubic Decimeter
1000 Cubic Decimeters	1 Cubic Meter

Conversion Table

Length x Width x Height or Depth

17 Wind Chill Chart

Wind	Temperature								
MPH	Degrees F								
Calm	40	35	30	25	20	15	10	5	0
5	36	31	25	19	13	7	1	-5	-11
10	34	27	21	15	9	3	-4	-10	-16
15	32	25	19	13	6	0	-7	-13	-19
20	30	24	17	11	4	-2	-9	-15	-22
25	29	23	16	9	3	-4	-11	-17	-24
30	28	22	15	8	1	-5	-12	-19	-26
35	28	21	14	7	0	-7	-14	-21	-27
40	27	20	13	6	1	-8	-15	-22	-29
45	26	19	12	5	-2	-9	-16	-23	-30
50	26	19	12	4	-3	-10	-17	-24	-31
55	25	18	11	4	-3	-11	-18	-25	-32
60	25	17	10	3	-4	-11	-18	-26	-33

Wind Chill Chart

18   Wind Speed

Wind Speed

Knots	KPH	MPH	Beaufort Scale
5	9.3	5.8	Light Breeze
10	18.5	11.5	Gentle Breeze
15	27.8	17.3	Moderate Breeze
20	37.1	23	Fresh Breeze
25	46.3	28.8	Strong Breeze
30	55.6	34.5	Near Gale
35	64.9	40.3	Gale
40	74.1	46	Gale
45	83.4	51.8	Strong Gale
50	92.7	57.5	Storm
55	101.9	63.3	Storm
60	111.2	69	Violent Storm
65	120.5	74.8	Hurricane

Wind Speed

MPH	KPH	Knots	Beaufort Scale
5	8	4.3	Light Breeze
10	16.1	8.7	Gentle Breeze
15	24.1	13	Moderate Breeze
20	32.2	17.4	Fresh Breeze
25	40.2	21.7	Strong Breeze
30	48.3	26.1	Strong Breeze
35	56.3	30.4	Near Gale
40	64.4	34.8	Gale
45	72.4	39.1	Gale
50	80.5	43.4	Strong Gale
55	88.5	47.8	Storm
60	96.6	52.1	Storm
65	104.6	56.5	Violent Storm
70	112.7	60.8	Violent Storm
75	120.7	65.2	Hurricane

19   Wire Gauge

Gauge	Inch	Millimeter
2	0.2625	6.668
2 1/2	0.253	6.43
3	0.2437	6.19
3 1/2	0.234	5.94
4	0.2253	5.723
4 1/2	0.216	5.49
5	0.207	5.258
5 1/2	0.2	5.08
6	0.192	4.877
6 1/2	0.184	4.67
7	0.177	4.496
7 1/2	0.17	4.32
8	0.162	4.115
8 1/2	0.155	3.94
9	0.1483	3.767
9 1/2	0.142	3.61
10	0.135	3.429
10 1/2	0.128	3.25
11	0.1205	3.061
11 1/2	0.113	2.87
12	0.1055	2.68
12 1/2	0.099	2.51

Warning

Always consult with professionals.

The information in this book is general.

Other factors can come into play.

Author

Some other books by William J Saunders
Available on Amazon.com

How to Buy New Windows for Your Home
The Home Improvement Guide
ISBN-13: 978-1982091507

How to Buy Replacement Windows for Your
Home
The Home Improvement Guide
ISBN-13: 978-1495257582

House Windows Vocabulary
A Glossary of Definitions
ISBN-13: 9781984126399

Math for Homeowners
Everyday Solutions
ISBN-13: 978-1985763937